SINCERE DALLIANCES
ISSUE #2

Sincere Dalliances
Issue #2

H.S. Leigh Koonce, Editor

Ellerslie Books

First Printing, 2023

Contents

Raining Again

Felix Alexander

It's raining again.
Just like last week.
I didn't mind the rain last week.
It was only a minor nuisance, a slight twist of fate that we laughed at.
But last week was different.
Last week was with you.

Yesterday, the counselors sat the marching band down in the school's
        auditorium
and told us what happened.
You, torn from our grasp by your own hands.
There was no music in the air that day.
The words, quietly spoken - almost whispered - dealt the loudest blow.

Tonight is the homecoming football game.
I can tell there is something in the air,
like that damp smell from tiny droplets burrowing into the ground -
petrichor, they call it - mixes with the sadness from the band
and the excitement from the students in the stands
to form some twisted new emotion.

Cheerleaders chant in vain (Let's go! Let's go!) but their wasted
    words
never quite reach us;
their high spirits never quite reach our souls, which are
higher still, up in the stands, eyes glued to the waxing moon, her
    three-quarter face
slashed open by thousands of raindrops.

Halftime approaches quickly.
We wipe the sweat away along with the blossoms of tears and warm
    up in silence.
After all, the show must go on.
Don't mess up, don't mess up,
I repeat in my head, because this was for you.
The only good thing about the rain is that no one can see you cry.

I'm not sure exactly when the raindrops become teardrops.
Salt from my eyes and sadness from the sky mix together
and dance down my skin, a confluence of two streams of sorrow.
I imagine the clouds are crying with us.

I'll have to hang up my band uniform in my room once more.
I remember when they had just finished drying, as if it was yesterday.
I don't want to think about yesterday.
But we can't leave our hearts out to dry.
It's not that easy.
If sadness could evaporate, the sun would be a god again.

The homecoming dance is tomorrow.
I won't be going, but I know people who will.
I can only imagine how strange that will feel.
Strange to be dancing so soon, suits shimmering like a tear.

Maybe tomorrow, everything will seem clearer.
Maybe the tears that blur my sight will be lifted off of my face

like the droplets on the sleeves of my uniform left in a warm patch
    of sun.
Maybe tomorrow, we will all dance together.
Until then, the rain will fall.

Night Shades in Troubled Times

Myrtle Thomas

the night draws me away into thoughts
into dreams in these quiet hours
the moon is my pillow the darkness my blanket
echoes of that summer night still resonate even now
they are my wings that carry me.

the sky is clear but my eyes cloudy with rain
and my chest rumbles with thunder
ravens tare at my heart and time is a tomb
an hourglass of pain with sand in my wounds
dreading the long winter days and nights.

will memories ever be enough until time erodes my mind?
I'm buried under a weeping willow like a root
feeling time dance in my limbs and my soul rings like a bell
my heart feels like a dead tree standing by the road
un-noticed and broken burned by your fire.

years play by me like a broken record plays in a soft wind

the melody like stones thrown against a window
the sound of ashes flung on a metal roof and the rain cries with me
and the autumn leaves change their clothes and turn their faces
I often wonder if the sky can see my sad eyes - watching it loom.

Rose/risenwood

Aja Bailey

Dog-eared sheet music rest on bony skilled fingers
perfumed in chlorine baths and riots of spring
amongst the heavenly light lint

Glistening sin on your shire
crafted by some old country man
Sugar gloss strum off your tips
scratches...strings
on my stomach
noteless and red and chords undefined

On stage there you are
one eye towards the rash ceiling
the other on her flush ash neck
No urge to play your skin built babe
though my sap out-scents hers
diffusing under God's feet

We could've made Broadway babies
during the interlude
or as the congregation ate Easter cake

A snail

Brandon Nicholas

See the way
I move
slow—
a snail

with one careful foot
in front of one captured foot.
I leave
a trail.
Without looking back, I feel
its languishing length.

To never grow—
to exist then, now, and over again
simultaneously,
interdependently.

It is always me you see—
each time the same snail
just a different shell.

The Catharsis

Gargi Sidana

A blurb of blue- oceanic breeze
Fat cucumber gingerly placed
On luxury shelves beneath the earth.
A swing of child's play- green meadows
Snoring in the layers of the earth
A cerulean cup - musky sky
Counting the thin crust of milky stars
A bucket of cries- The Rain
Pouring/ galloping the scarlet razor-grass
Bunch of old boys swirling in its hue
Siblings dancing on their shoulders- twigs of heart
Pinnacle of beauty- Daffodils
Hopped on the bumblebee
Grinning teeth- sodden petals
Whizzing chores of ballad
Nightingale burst into tears,
The liquid greenish haze- An owl,
Hooting at the crimson lips of the night
Slumber cheeks of the brook
Coursing through my blood
Mosaic veins of thy rocks- Mountains

Slipping through the creaks of the buildings
The wide mouth of the beast- Valleys
Crawling over the catharsis of the algae
Slipping! Tumbling! Rumbling
Earth is crumbling!
Human caprice wrecks the mantles
Nature gleams the temples

it was loki

Linda M. Crates

they taught me
loving you was wrong,
they taught me that
i was nothing without
their god;
and they taught me the rapture
may happen at any moment—

but now i realize that love
is love and she comes in many
beautiful forms,
and loving you was never wrong;

i realized i have magic and talents
and gifts that i deserve to harness and
become better at—

i am trying to learn to live a life
where i don't live in fear,
and i have walked away from their
churches because it was never

their god that comforted me when i
was crying;

it was loki.

Thanks Karen

Angie Brady

"You know, my sister doesn't have any kids and she is having just the best time. She travels and her music is really taking off." The woman was tall with a pinched face, and her bright, sickly sweet smile made Emma wonder if they were related by blood or marriage. Hopefully marriage.

Thanks Karen, but your sister is an unemployed narcissist who likely has a drug problem.

"Thanks Dorea. Will you excuse me," Emma said instead, smile brittle. Turning around she made a beeline for the bathroom, it being as good of an excuse as any to escape the same goddamn conversation over and over again.

Walking past Johnathan, she automatically reached out to skim her fingers along his forearm. His hand turned to grab hers, but she was already past him, so he turned to wink at her instead. She grinned back, then Aunt Jodi abruptly brought his attention back to her with her wild Italian hand gestures.

Once behind the safety of the bathroom door Emma splashed some water on her face, mentally debating how much longer they had to stay at the reunion.

"There she is, little Emma Bear. Where's the new hubby?"

Obviously not in the fucking women's restroom.

"I'm sure you saw Johnathan out there, LeeAnn." Emma leaned back against the cool tile wall, crossing her arms to face her older cousin. LeeAnn had on her typical short skirt with a jean jacket she refused to admit had gone out of style a decade ago. But she was pretty and had the confidence to pull it off, which irked Emma more than it maybe should have. One of the many rings LeeAnn wore tinkled on her glass when she took a sip of her cocktail.

"Did you really have to bring a drink into the bathroom?"

"You know what they say, never leave your drink unattended. Here, hold it for me."

And somehow Emma ended up with the tall, pink drink in her hand, side wet with condensation and black straw just tipping out over the rim. Rolling her eyes, she silently waited for the woman to emerge from the stall and wash her hands. To think, they'd been best friends for years back in the day.

"Here, I have to get back," she finally said, thrusting the glass at her cousin when she'd thrown away the crumpled paper towel.

"Hmmm. No. I think you need that."

You probably also think your makeup is subtle.

"I really don't. I'm driving home soon." She tried to hand the glass back again, but with no success.

"So how are things? Heard about your....problems." Her eyes flicked down to Emma's stomach and up again.

Who knew there were questions worse than "when are you having kids?"

"We're fine," she said resolutely, raising her chin a fraction. But then her face fell in confusion when LeeAnn rolled her eyes.

"Like hell you are," she said. She gestured at the glass still sweating in Emma's hand. "Throw that, it'll help some."

A strangled chuckle escaped before Emma realized her cousin was not kidding.

She's insane.

"You're insane, I'm not doing that."

"Why not? Haven't you been ready to explode since before you walked in the door?"

Yes.

"No." Emma started toward the door, ready for the conversation to be over. But LeeAnn took a step to stand right in front of it.

"Hmmm let's see. Which one is the worst? Oh, how about the pitying looks from the old ladies who call you a 'poor dear.'"

Those are the least of my problems.

"No. Move."

LeeAnn tapped her chin with a forefinger. "Oh I know, the ones who are too afraid to bring it up and practically strain themselves to avoid saying the word 'baby.'"

Okay, they are pretty annoying.

"What is wrong with you?"

LeeAnna ignored her again. "Then it must be the ones who try to help with their amazing miracle stories. Oh wait, even better, the stories about people who are just so damn happy by themselves."

Alright, you really need to shut up now.

Emma's stomach was in knots and she really didn't know what to do with the glass in her hand since LeeAnn refused to take it. Tossing back her hair she tried for nonchalance, ignoring the brief warble in her voice. "Are we 8 years old again? I said. Move. Now."

"There you go, let that anger out, darling. If those idiots aren't the ones eating at you it must be the happy ones. The ones that have their happy ending."

I can't do this.

"Stop."

"The announcements all over Instagram about a baby being born. Or conceived. You know, the ones bragging that they didn't use a condom."

Yes, of course I know. How can anyone not know. It's the only thing anyone talks about.

"Alright! I get it!"

"Now we are getting-"

"My god SHUT UP! Are you happy now? Yes I'm angry and now I'm yelling and yes I'm FUCKING MISERABLE." She took a step forward until she was in LeeAnn's personal space and a drop of condensation from the drink dropped and fell next to the perfectly manicured toes peeking out of her sandals. "Now get out of my way." Her voice turned calm and quiet but shook with force.

LeeAnn moved her face an inch closer until her breath ghosted across her chin and enunciated, "Throw it."

And in one motion Emma turned and threw the glass against the wall, ice and glass ricocheting in every direction. She didn't even realize she'd made a noise until the guttural shout echoed back at her. She didn't know if there was alcohol or tears on her cheeks - but one way or another her face was damp and she was panting, trying to catch her breath.

Her mind quickly caught up with her body and she drew her arms around her waist, not proud of the break in her control. The one thing she could do was hold herself together, and now it seemed like even that wasn't true.

I'm a fucking mess.

LeeAnn stepped in front of her, tissue extended, eyes suddenly soft. "You're not okay. But that's okay, you will be. Just not right now. Right now you're..."

"A fucking mess," Emma finished with a shaky exhale, looking away.

"You said it, not me," LeeAnn said with a smile. "It's okay to not be okay. Throw things. Break things. Spend an ungodly amount of money on a new purse. Skip work and stay in bed all day. Grieve. You can't start healing until you do."

The tears started again, and Emma did her best to will them away. So she nodded, not sure if she actually agreed but absolutely sure she wanted the other woman to leave.

Now get out so I can have a good cry.

"If you use the side door no one will see you leave. I'll send that hunky husband of yours out after you."

LeeAnn walked away, but hesitated with a hand on the door. "Call anytime. You're not the only one dealing with shit like this."

Before Emma could turn around to see her cousin, she was gone. And Emma put her forehead on the door and cried, the smell of rum and coconut encompassing the small room.

It

Mars Gray

Rip my essence from me and force me to stare at it.
Because I cannot bear to
Not in photographs, not in the mirror I will scratch at it, surface deep,
    until the glitter flakes
and fades away

Because that's all it was, nothing truly special, nothing permanent
I never get beyond the first layer before the sheer force of whatever 'it'
    is overwhelms me

I will lie on a lab table under the fluorescent lights hate so much, if you
promise to be honest
about what you see beneath my skin
Crack my rib cage open like lightning cleaves the sky
Pan for gold in the rivers of my veins

Take 'it' in your hand, shining under those awful lights and show
    it to me
I won't force you to tell me 'it's' still pretty
But I would love it if you did

Queen Mount

Aja Bailey

Some time 'round 2:15ish I'm sick of the bleeding
I lift up black faded cursive leaves
on the modern headboard
heaven bound
to the jeweled oiled Black magic
I watch my other self

Stir beneath a blue deep quilt with mint streaks
         Lake Nyasa
Body stink of sweat and Luster's Pink lotion
      Date palms and flamingo shit or nearby pollution
The rumble of the train 500 kilometers away
       A hippo or two run over ashy ground
Cheap ceiling fan whips the wind on my slick paint face
     a summer breeze against bronze honey
Earrings, wrap, canvas, continent of gold
  I am a sanctuary
away from boring home bones and cramps and colonial anger
I dodge mommyhood
 I taste motherland

Father's wisdom

Brandon Nicholas

He said:
In any given relationship
there is one who loves the other more.
Always.

He was right
Is

But what he forgot to mention
is that the scales will sway—
sometimes unknowingly,
and if you don't know who loves who more
anymore
be wary.

Bless

Mars Gray

Bless this broken land
This dirt that has been rearranged to fit the wants of foreigners
These mountains that have been carved up and taken from
These rivers that no one was supposed to cross

Bless the things that have found sanctuary and spirit here, that any self
    proclaimed
'respectable baptist church' wouldn't let through the front doors on
        a sunday
Or any other day of the week for that matter
Bless the sun kissed forest floors
The slippery river rocks every babe has tripped over in their eagerness
        at least once
And bless the long tunnels in the deep earth, running through the
        stone like veins bled dry

Little Bird Resting in my Heart

Myrtle Thomas

darling have you not known
that my heart is full of ravens and humming birds?
oceans of stars and heavens of darkness
and you swimming in the depths!

I can love you in my kisses and the wide river
that winds through my heart   the wings -
of my soul and every shadow that crossed my path
all of my life that has been or could be.

even when the waters of our love are brooding
and the waves wrestle against us - there we still are
looking into the rain and swimming in each other
comparing thunder to rainbows and feeling the lightening.

we are like two birds in the rain cowering on a branch
of red and gold fire - our eyes on the morning sky
our wings wet from the journey of love
O' little bird that sings in my heart!

Moons, Fireflies, Slugs, and Moths

Mars Gray

"I don't know what to do when I'm angry."
I tell the moon hanging in the sky.
In my head I imagine she started the conversation by asking me why I
was crying.
"I hate being angry like this. Like I could tear the world apart if I
felt like it."
I tell the lightning bugs winking at me from the tree line.
In my head I imagine they're dancing in the twilight shadows, trying to
remind me there's
wonder in the world.
"Anger is an ugly, bloody thing."
I tell the slugs slowly meandering on the sidewalk in front of me.
In my head I imagine they're just happy to have company on their night
time stroll.
"What can someone so young do with so much anger?"
I ask the moths crowding around the porch light.
I imagine they're like me, trying desperately to have something they've
mistaken for
something else.

Siren Song

Felix Alexander

Come to me, O ship on the sea, come to my misty shore.
We, the sirens, will drag you with daydreams down to the ocean floor.
We'll sing you to sleep and you'll wake up on your deathbed.

Twisted dreams lead to piercing screams, from fantasy to horror.
We'll tantalize you with visions of kalaidoscopic clusters of coral.
Come to me, O ship on the sea, come to my misty shore.

Your hopes for paradise turn the water deep red.
Shipwrecks litter the path of the fools we've led.
We'll sing you to sleep and you'll wake up in your deathbed.

So tie yourself to the mast and cover your ears, but do be warned -
you won't be the last to face your fears; every warning you've ignored.
So come to me, O ship on the sea, come to my misty shore.

Storms will come and lightning will flash, but 'tis not thunder you
    should dread.
It's a pity for you that you haven't already turned and fled.
We'll sing you to sleep and you'll wake up on your deathbed.

So while your foolish self does naively sleep and snore,
We'll be ready to drag you down, deep into the ocean floor.

Come to me, O ship on the sea, come to my misty shore.
We'll sing you to sleep and you'll wake up in your deathbed,
just like all the fools before.

The Night's Eyeless Face
and I'm but a Dream

Myrtle Thomas

I recall the night's face and its dark garment
  and the starlight in his eyes dancing like silver dust
he comes to me like a star shimmering in the darkness
  and I rest for a while on the wings of the night.

How vast is the extent of the universe holding-
  the cosmic thoughts of my dreams or the reality
of yearning to trespass the realm that I fear and long for
the trails of a shooting star as it burns beyond my eyes.

There were times that my mind troubled the moonlight
  searching for the shadows that hide from my eyes
and the wind that dances with his voice as it takes my breath
  maybe I chase after the night while it flees from me.

Time extends the length of the universe and the stars
  and it's then that he comes on the hem of the night's robe
to rest on my sleeping shoulders and to kiss my quiet sighs
  if only I could find the path of the burning star trailing after him.

In wonderment I grieve and yearn for that path that leads away
into the setting of the starlit night and his kiss that calls to me
from the shadows of cosmic existence in my temporal eyes and mind
as a residual ghost that comes to me in-between sunlight and
moonlight.

now it seems worse

Linda M. Crate

i remember
when my classmate threatened to
shoot me and another girl,
his mother called me a liar;
even though there were eyewitnesses—
all because i was nervous,
i didn't want to be in the same
room with him;

i was in fifth grade when this
happened and it is not something
i can forget—

nor will i ever forget the boy that
was expelled for having a hit list,
but i don't know who was on it;
he was always pretty quiet so that

was a terrifying discovery
and the school wouldn't release the list—

but i never had to have active shooter
drills,
i was never shot at in a cafeteria
or in a class room;

i never had to smear blood on my body
and play dead so i wouldn't be shot—

america always had guns,
but now it seems worse;
as if the violence and the rage are
out of control and understanding
and empathy are in short supply.

Bruise Royals

Aja Bailey

In your sleep you asked for something plump
I gave you a plum

I meant you.
Where would your juices take me?

Probably where love is out of range twined in
misheard letters as the dead-nettles meets the bruise
royals and blues somewhere between the p's and hues

Organized organisms

Brandon Nicholas

Organized organisms,
roots of unknown origin,
with brutish strength
vault unappreciative limbs up through the earth
into the free air.
Scoffing upon the shoulders of their underground brethren.
Shaking in the wind.
Singing their vanity.
Until their height betrays them,
and the cold creeps down from the clouds
and bites their heads
and they fall to the ground—
some lifeless, some shamed.
They burrow themselves back into the earth's womb
in search of solace among their estranged kin.
The cycle begins again.

A bug on the moon

Brandon Nicholas

What would this vermin do
if it caught
the Moon?

Watch it
crash on the
incandescent
surface
buzzing
furiously
unsatisfied
and burning
until it
leaps away
to find
another moon.
But not before
it is sucked back
into the first's
gravitational pull
again and again,
rendering it

flightless—
A
hopeless
satellite
for the remainder
of its life

—or
until someone
turns off
the light.

petals or darts

Aja Bailey

Why am I still reaching for heaven when my prayers burn to confetti
and sanded to aimless adjectives?

Have they been poured into twin hourglasses?
One hanging at the entrance of a contemporary Hell.
Another on my enemy's desk next to the portrait of his boo.
Or have they been dusted on candy cantaloupes in a rosé melamine
bowl for the sweet and sinless palates?

I ask God to break my compass
and smash the dial to glitter for fuzzy jackets worn by badder bitches.
Turn the gold scraps into beads for my ombré box braids and give
those petal darts back to the Greek sky

I don't want a damn destination anymore

As Shadows Fall in Haunting Clarity

Myrtle Thomas

I've looked in all of the secret places
between the sunlight and the night's shadows
in the hidden realms of time and portals
deep in daydreams and dreams from pillows.

I've listened to each whisper and the echo of air
straining my ears and my head is faint
the wind holds you for only so long then you're gone
gone except from my haunting memory.

this thirst lingers as long as I strive to breathe
my breast is consumed with hunger and pain
tears find my lips as they long for that unforgotten kiss
even as these dreams fade from my mind and my sleep cries.

through my windows there are no longer flowers nor sun
no light penetrates from the moon as clouds hang on my head
desiring the rain and thunder to drown me in this grief
this thirst never fades, nor my breast drained of desire.

I hold onto that first tremble in your arms as it was a quake
a thunder as if the sky was falling as the light in your eyes died
now that look has left from my eyes and I'm blind without you
deaf and mute in the earth's light and numb to the air touching me

shinrin-yoku

Brandon Nicholas

I went into the woods
to bury my shoes.
To plant roots, raise limbs, and
dance with trees
to the applause of leaves
while god-winds blow
through what winter left of me.

two periods in two weeks

Aja Bailey

I missed you harder than you ever got but she still mourned the kids
we were supposed to home outside the puss baguette
and she cried the wounds that bled from your mouth when
I carried away your tongue holding our next names
You will not taste my budding bliss while craving and panting
for other offspring in mountains like dogs in dirt luxury

feared your rejection

Linda M. Crates

pink sunsets,
white roses,
vnv nation, kate bush,
star trek, repo! the genetic
opera, the rocky horror
picture show;

all still sing to me of
your name—

the other day when i was walking with
my mother and fizzy in linesville,
a purple butterfly whizzed by;

i thought you of you when i went to visit
you that one time in edinboro—

and i cannot help but wonder of the faerie
that woke in me the dreaming when i thought
magic had died in me for the last time,

i didn't know it would rise again on different
and new wings;

thank you for waking the phoenix spirit in me—

i hope you are doing well wherever you are,
maybe i shouldn't but i still miss you;
i didn't know how to tell you i fell in love
with you because i feared your rejection.

Rain

Mars Gray

It's dark out today
Dull and tired
Nothing is particularly wrong
My bones need a minute to rest
Head on the glass
Watching the rain
Wishing it was on my skin
Wind and rain wash most things clean
But it won't ever reach the things that need to see the sun

let society crumble

Linda M. Crates

i have waited my whole life,
but i am done waiting;

i am going to find the parts
of me that i left behind
when i was trying to please people

sew them back into the galaxy
of my stars and moons and suns,
plant the flowers back in my
garden and watch them grow taller
than the oaks and pines and maples;

maybe even taller than a redwood—

go find the birds that are still living,
and invite them back to the new forest
of my heart;

i am done taking myself for granted—

and i am going to reclaim my voice,
my magic, and myself and never ever
let anyone break me again;

i will shatter them with my light before
they break me with their darkness

because i surrender to no one—

my heart is mine,
and i fear not my power
or my magic any longer;
so they have no power over me—

let society crumble, sometimes they are too cruel.

Falling and Rotting

Mars Gray

i'm not falling apart

falling apart insinuates some kind of mistake

a building constructed on a faulty foundation

falling apart implies some kind of profound purpose to no longer
    existing

i am rotting

rotting is much less admirable

rotting is decaying slowly, being eaten alive from within

and it only shows on the outside when it's too late to do anything
    about it

falling apart is a beautiful tragedy

like Rome or Athens

rotting is repulsive and pitiful like a diseased tree or roadkill

Autumn Walks in the Twilight

Myrtle Thomas

*

how my love we are tangled in this life !
bound by heart and bone   earth and air
the love that lives in this ancient skin
this thing we can not control - the feelings
when we were new.

**

even now in my autumn there is still spring
the seasons where life is green and golden
where the brown and green hues still rise-
in your earthen eyes and I'm the sky
when time only is the clouds.

***

O' the gladness I find in your eyes and laughter
and I bless the earth from which you came
and praise your mother and father for this gift to me
this light that is a lamp into my heart -

and a moon in my darkness.

****

such a strange day when I found you - like an autumn leaf
a song that can never be forgotten or a breath that finds itself
I've imprisoned your love in the ocean of my heart
darling are we not the earth and the sky ? together we are
I've captured the flowers of your lips.

*****

have we lost nothing but time as it sheds its skin?
but one day these memories will fade and disappear
for like rain it falls and is seen and evaporates into the air
darling we are but a butterfly winging in the wind silently
evading the moment when time ceases.

******

O' twilight cover me in your memory and bury me in his heart
for we will one day be lost in an unseen portal
we can't know this sequence of time nor taste this fate
nor continue in the theme of our love and our life
but we lean our ears to the whispering time.

****

no one hears our whispering hearts nor our longing sighs
nor sees what lives within our breath no one !
no one knows we speak to each other without speaking
or do they see the stars we hold in our hands as an offering
no one knows that I could never speak to another.

Contributors

Felix Alexander is a junior at Jefferson High School, where he is active in band, chorus, and acting. He has long been interested in writing, especially after attending the WV Governor's School for the Arts for creative writing.

Aja Bailey is a writer and serial napper residing in the eastern panhandle of West Virginia. Her work has appeared in *West Trade Review*, *Malasaña*, *Duende*, *Gambling the Aisle*, and *Backbone Mountain Review*.

Angie Brady was born and raised in Northeast PA and lives a quiet life at home with her husband and son. When she is procrastinating writing she'll likely be found reading or playing board games with friends.

Linda M. Crate (she/her) is a Pennsylvanian writer whose poetry, short stories, articles, and reviews have been published in a myriad of magazines both online and in print. She has twelve published chapbooks the latest being: *Searching Stained Glass Windows For An Answer* (Alien Buddha Publishing, December 2022). She is also the author of the novella *Mates* (Alien Buddha Publishing, March 2022). Her debut book of photography *Songs of the Creek* (Alien Buddha Publishing, April 2023) was recently published.

Mars Gray aka Gold Fielding is a queer Appalachian artist who takes great pride in his roots and history. His favorite era of art is Impressionism (specifically Monet) and the Rococo Period. They want to be a studio/fine arts professor when they grow up.

Brandon Nicholas is native to West Virginia where he attended Shepherd University. He is a father, poet, and bartender.

Gargi Sidana

Myrtle Thomas has been published in *Otherwise Engaged Literature and Arts Journal, The Writers and Readers Magazine, Lothlorien Poetry Journal, Lothlorien Poetry Blog,* and *Masticadores USA Blog.* She self published four poetry books and is a member of Allpoetry.com, pen name Blue2U. She lives in the USA.

www.ingramcontent.com/pod-product-compliance
Lightning Source LLC
Chambersburg PA
CBHW061642130726
47996CB00003B/1411